This Planner Belongs To:

_____

_____

_____

September 2019

Sunday	Monday	Tuesday	Wednesday	Thursday	Friday	Saturday
1	2	3	4	5	6	7
8	9	10	11	12	13	14
15	16	17	18	19	20	21
22	23	24	25	26	27	28
29	30	1	2	3	4	5

"Inspiration and genius—one and the same."

~*Victor Hugo*

September

09/02/19 to 09/08/19

○ 2.MONDAY

○ 3.TUESDAY

○ 4.WEDNESDAY

○ 5.THURSDAY

○ 6.FRIDAY

○ 7.SATURDAY / 8.SUNDAY

PRIORITIES

TO DO

September

09/09/19 to 09/15/19

○ 9.MONDAY

PRIORITIES

○ 10.TUESDAY

○ 11.WEDNESDAY

TO DO

○ 12.THURSDAY

○ 13.FRIDAY

○ 14.SATURDAY / 15.SUNDAY

September

Week 38

○ 16 MONDAY

PRIORITIES

○ 17. TUESDAY

○ 18. WEDNESDAY

TO DO

○ 19. THURSDAY

○ 20. FRIDAY

○ 21 SATURDAY / 22 SUNDAY

September

○ 23. MONDAY

PRIORITIES

○ 24. TUESDAY

○ 25. WEDNESDAY

TO DO

○ 26. THURSDAY

○ 27. FRIDAY

○ 28. SATURDAY / 29. SUNDAY

September

Week 40   09/30/19 to 10/06/19

○ 30.MONDAY

PRIORITIES

○ 1TUESDAY

○ 2WEDNESDAY

TO DO

○ 3THURSDAY

○ 4.FRIDAY

○ 5.SATURDAY / 6SUNDAY

October 2019

Sunday	Monday	Tuesday	Wednesday	Thursday	Friday	Saturday
29	30	1	2	3	4	5
6	7	8	9	10	11	12
13	14	15	16	17	18	19
20	21	22	23	24	25	26
27	28	29	30	31	1	2

"A short saying oft contains much wisdom." ~*Sophocles*

October

10/07/19 to 10/13/19

○ 7.MONDAY

PRIORITIES

○ 8.TUESDAY

○ 9.WEDNESDAY

TO DO

○ 10.THURSDAY

○ 11.FRIDAY

○ 12.SATURDAY / 13.SUNDAY

October

Week 42   10/14/19 to 10/20/19

○ 14.MONDAY

PRIORITIES

_____

_____

○ 15.TUESDAY

_____

_____

_____

_____

○ 16.WEDNESDAY

TO DO

_____

_____

○ 17.THURSDAY

_____

_____

_____

_____

○ 18.FRIDAY

_____

_____

_____

_____

○ 19.SATURDAY / 20.SUNDAY

_____

_____

_____

_____

October

○ 21 MONDAY

PRIORITIES

○ 22. TUESDAY

○ 23. WEDNESDAY

TO DO

○ 24. THURSDAY

○ 25. FRIDAY

○ 26. SATURDAY / 27 SUNDAY

October

○ 28. MONDAY

PRIORITIES

○ 29. TUESDAY

○ 30. WEDNESDAY

TO DO

○ 31. THURSDAY

○ 1 FRIDAY

○ 2 SATURDAY / 3 SUNDAY

November 2019

Sunday	Monday	Tuesday	Wednesday	Thursday	Friday	Saturday
27	28	29	30	31	1	2
3	4	5	6	7	8	9
10	11	12	13	14	15	16
17	18	19	20	21	22	23
24	25	26	27	28	29	30

"Sooner or later, those who win are those that think they can."

~Paul Tournier

November

Week 45

○ 4.MONDAY

PRIORITIES

○ 5.TUESDAY

○ 6.WEDNESDAY

TO DO

○ 7.THURSDAY

○ 8.FRIDAY

○ 9.SATURDAY / 10.SUNDAY

November

Week 46　　　　　　　　　　　　　　　11/11/19 to 11/17/19

○ 11 MONDAY

PRIORITIES

○ 12 TUESDAY

○ 13 WEDNESDAY

TO DO

○ 14 THURSDAY

○ 15 FRIDAY

○ 16 SATURDAY / 17 SUNDAY

November

○ 18. MONDAY

○ 19. TUESDAY

PRIORITIES

○ 20. WEDNESDAY

TO DO

○ 21. THURSDAY

○ 22. FRIDAY

○ 23. SATURDAY / 24. SUNDAY

November

○ 25. MONDAY

PRIORITIES

○ 26. TUESDAY

○ 27. WEDNESDAY

TO DO

○ 28. THURSDAY

○ 29. FRIDAY

○ 30. SATURDAY / 1 SUNDAY

December 2019

Sunday	Monday	Tuesday	Wednesday	Thursday	Friday	Saturday
1	2	3	4	5	6	7
8	9	10	11	12	13	14
15	16	17	18	19	20	21
22	23	24	25	26	27	28
29	30	31	1	2	3	4

"The three great essentials to achieve anything worthwhile are: Hard work, Stick-to-itiveness, and Common sense."

~ Thomas A. Edison

December

○ 2.MONDAY

PRIORITIES

○ 3.TUESDAY

○ 4.WEDNESDAY

TO DO

○ 5.THURSDAY

○ 6.FRIDAY

○ 7.SATURDAY / 8.SUNDAY

December

12/09/19 to 12/15/19

○ 9.MONDAY

PRIORITIES

○ 10.TUESDAY

○ 11.WEDNESDAY

TO DO

○ 12.THURSDAY

○ 13.FRIDAY

○ 14.SATURDAY / 15.SUNDAY

December

○ 16.MONDAY

○ 17.TUESDAY

○ 18.WEDNESDAY

○ 19.THURSDAY

○ 20.FRIDAY

○ 21.SATURDAY / 22.SUNDAY

PRIORITIES

TO DO

December

12/23/19 to 12/29/19

○ 23. MONDAY

PRIORITIES

_____

_____

_____

○ 24. TUESDAY

_____

_____

_____

_____

○ 25. WEDNESDAY

TO DO

_____

○ 26. THURSDAY

_____

_____

_____

○ 27. FRIDAY

_____

_____

_____

○ 28. SATURDAY / 29. SUNDAY

_____

_____

_____

December

○ 30.MONDAY

PRIORITIES

○ 31TUESDAY

○ 1WEDNESDAY

TO DO

○ 2THURSDAY

○ 3FRIDAY

○ 4.SATURDAY / 5SUNDAY

January 2020

Sunday	Monday	Tuesday	Wednesday	Thursday	Friday	Saturday
29	30	31	1	2	3	4
5	6	7	8	9	10	11
12	13	14	15	16	17	18
19	20	21	22	23	24	25
26	27	28	29	30	31	1

"How am I going to live today in order to create the tomorrow I'm committed to?" ~*Tony Robbins*

January

○ 6.MONDAY

PRIORITIES

○ 7.TUESDAY

○ 8.WEDNESDAY

TO DO

○ 9.THURSDAY

○ 10.FRIDAY

○ 11.SATURDAY / 12.SUNDAY

January

○ 13 MONDAY

PRIORITIES

○ 14 TUESDAY

○ 15 WEDNESDAY

TO DO

○ 16 THURSDAY

○ 17 FRIDAY

○ 18 SATURDAY / 19 SUNDAY

January

○ 20.MONDAY

PRIORITIES

○ 21.TUESDAY

○ 22.WEDNESDAY

TO DO

○ 23.THURSDAY

○ 24.FRIDAY

○ 25.SATURDAY / 26.SUNDAY

January

○ 27. MONDAY

PRIORITIES

○ 28. TUESDAY

○ 29. WEDNESDAY

TO DO

○ 30. THURSDAY

○ 31 FRIDAY

○ 1 SATURDAY / 2 SUNDAY

February 2020

Sunday	Monday	Tuesday	Wednesday	Thursday	Friday	Saturday
26	27	28	29	30	31	1
2	3	4	5	6	7	8
9	10	11	12	13	14	15
16	17	18	19	20	21	22
23	24	25	26	27	28	29

"If you owe the bank $100 that's your problem. If you owe the bank $100 million, that's the bank's problem." ~J. Paul Getty

February

○ 3.MONDAY

PRIORITIES

○ 4.TUESDAY

○ 5.WEDNESDAY

TO DO

○ 6.THURSDAY

○ 7.FRIDAY

○ 8.SATURDAY / 9.SUNDAY

February

○ 10 MONDAY

PRIORITIES

○ 11 TUESDAY

○ 12 WEDNESDAY

TO DO

○ 13 THURSDAY

○ 14 FRIDAY

○ 15 SATURDAY / 16 SUNDAY

February

Week 8   02/17/20 to 02/23/20

○ 17.MONDAY

○ 18.TUESDAY

○ 19.WEDNESDAY

TO DO

○ 20.THURSDAY

○ 21.FRIDAY

○ 22.SATURDAY / 23.SUNDAY

February

02/24/20 to 03/01/20

○ 24.MONDAY

PRIORITIES

○ 25.TUESDAY

○ 26.WEDNESDAY

TO DO

○ 27.THURSDAY

○ 28.FRIDAY

○ 29.SATURDAY / 1SUNDAY

March 2020

Sunday	Monday	Tuesday	Wednesday	Thursday	Friday	Saturday
1	2	3	4	5	6	7
8	9	10	11	12	13	14
15	16	17	18	19	20	21
22	23	24	25	26	27	28
29	30	31	1	2	3	4

"Every day I get up and look through the Forbes list of the richest people in America. If I'm not there, I go to work."

~Robert Orben

March

○ 2.MONDAY

PRIORITIES

○ 3.TUESDAY

○ 4.WEDNESDAY

TO DO

○ 5.THURSDAY

○ 6.FRIDAY

○ 7.SATURDAY / 8.SUNDAY

March

Week 1   03/09/20 to 03/15/20

○ 9.MONDAY

PRIORITIES

○ 10.TUESDAY

○ 11.WEDNESDAY

TO DO

○ 12.THURSDAY

○ 13.FRIDAY

○ 14.SATURDAY / 15.SUNDAY

March

○ 16.MONDAY

PRIORITIES

○ 17.TUESDAY

○ 18.WEDNESDAY

TO DO

○ 19.THURSDAY

○ 20.FRIDAY

○ 21.SATURDAY / 22.SUNDAY

March

○ 23.MONDAY

PRIORITIES

○ 24.TUESDAY

○ 25.WEDNESDAY

TO DO

○ 26.THURSDAY

○ 27.FRIDAY

○ 28.SATURDAY / 29.SUNDAY

March

Week 14

03/30/20 to 04/05/20

○ 30.MONDAY

○ 31.TUESDAY

○ 1.WEDNESDAY

○ 2.THURSDAY

○ 3.FRIDAY

○ 4.SATURDAY / 5.SUNDAY

PRIORITIES

TO DO

April 2020

Sunday	Monday	Tuesday	Wednesday	Thursday	Friday	Saturday
29	30	31	1	2	3	4
5	6	7	8	9	10	11
12	13	14	15	16	17	18
19	20	21	22	23	24	25
26	27	28	29	30	1	2

"I get to play golf for a living. What more could you ask for –
getting paid for what you love." ~ *Tiger Woods*

April

04/06/20 to 04/12/20

○ 6.MONDAY

PRIORITIES

○ 7.TUESDAY

○ 8.WEDNESDAY

TO DO

○ 9.THURSDAY

○ 10.FRIDAY

○ 11.SATURDAY / 12.SUNDAY

April

04/13/20 to 04/19/20

○ 13 MONDAY

PRIORITIES

○ 14 TUESDAY

○ 15 WEDNESDAY

TO DO

○ 16 THURSDAY

○ 17 FRIDAY

○ 18 SATURDAY / 19 SUNDAY

April

○ 20.MONDAY

PRIORITIES

○ 21.TUESDAY

○ 22.WEDNESDAY

TO DO

○ 23.THURSDAY

○ 24.FRIDAY

○ 25.SATURDAY / 26.SUNDAY

April

Week 18

04/27/20 to 05/03/20

○ 27. MONDAY

PRIORITIES

_____

_____

_____

○ 28. TUESDAY

_____

_____

_____

○ 29. WEDNESDAY

TO DO

_____

○ 30. THURSDAY

_____

_____

_____

_____

○ 1 FRIDAY

_____

_____

_____

_____

○ 2 SATURDAY / 3 SUNDAY

_____

_____

_____

May 2020

Sunday	Monday	Tuesday	Wednesday	Thursday	Friday	Saturday
26	27	28	29	30	1	2
3	4	5	6	7	8	9
10	11	12	13	14	15	16
17	18	19	20	21	22	23
24	25	26	27	28	29	30
31	1	2	3	4	5	6

"If you don't drive your business, you will be driven out of business."

~B. C. Forbes

May

Week 19

○ 4.MONDAY

PRIORITIES

○ 5.TUESDAY

○ 6.WEDNESDAY

TO DO

○ 7.THURSDAY

○ 8.FRIDAY

○ 9.SATURDAY / 10.SUNDAY

May

05/11/20 to 05/17/20

○ 11 MONDAY

PRIORITIES

○ 12 TUESDAY

○ 13 WEDNESDAY

TO DO

○ 14 THURSDAY

○ 15 FRIDAY

○ 16 SATURDAY / 17 SUNDAY

May

Week 21

05/18/20 to 05/24/20

○ 18.MONDAY

○ 19.TUESDAY

○ 20.WEDNESDAY

○ 21.THURSDAY

○ 22.FRIDAY

○ 23.SATURDAY / 24.SUNDAY

PRIORITIES

TO DO

May

Week 22

05/25/20 to 05/31/20

○ 25. MONDAY

PRIORITIES

○ 26. TUESDAY

○ 27. WEDNESDAY

TO DO

○ 28. THURSDAY

○ 29. FRIDAY

○ 30. SATURDAY / 31 SUNDAY

June 2020

Sunday	Monday	Tuesday	Wednesday	Thursday	Friday	Saturday
31	1	2	3	4	5	6
7	8	9	10	11	12	13
14	15	16	17	18	19	20
21	22	23	24	25	26	27
28	29	30	1	2	3	4

_____

_____

_____

_____

"If you listen to your fears. You will die never knowing what a great person you might have been." ~*Robert H. Schuller*

June

Week 23

○ 1 MONDAY

PRIORITIES

○ 2 TUESDAY

○ 3 WEDNESDAY

TO DO

○ 4 THURSDAY

○ 5 FRIDAY

○ 6 SATURDAY / 7 SUNDAY

June

○ 8.MONDAY

PRIORITIES

○ 9.TUESDAY

○ 10.WEDNESDAY

TO DO

○ 11.THURSDAY

○ 12.FRIDAY

○ 13.SATURDAY / 14.SUNDAY

June

○ 15.MONDAY

PRIORITIES

○ 16.TUESDAY

○ 17.WEDNESDAY

TO DO

○ 18.THURSDAY

○ 19.FRIDAY

○ 20.SATURDAY / 21.SUNDAY

June

06/22/20 to 06/28/20

○ 22.MONDAY

PRIORITIES

○ 23.TUESDAY

○ 24.WEDNESDAY

TO DO

○ 25.THURSDAY

○ 26.FRIDAY

○ 27.SATURDAY / 28.SUNDAY

June

○ 29.MONDAY

○ 30.TUESDAY

○ 1.WEDNESDAY

○ 2.THURSDAY

○ 3.FRIDAY

○ 4.SATURDAY / 5.SUNDAY

PRIORITIES

TO DO

July 2020

Sunday	Monday	Tuesday	Wednesday	Thursday	Friday	Saturday
28	29	30	1	2	3	4
5	6	7	8	9	10	11
12	13	14	15	16	17	18
19	20	21	22	23	24	25
26	27	28	29	30	31	1

"What the mind of man can conceive and believe, he can achieve." *~Napolean Hill*

July

○ 6.MONDAY

PRIORITIES

○ 7.TUESDAY

○ 8.WEDNESDAY

TO DO

○ 9.THURSDAY

○ 10.FRIDAY

○ 11.SATURDAY / 12.SUNDAY

July

○ 13 MONDAY

PRIORITIES

○ 14 TUESDAY

○ 15 WEDNESDAY

TO DO

○ 16 THURSDAY

○ 17 FRIDAY

○ 18 SATURDAY / 19 SUNDAY

July

○ 20.MONDAY

PRIORITIES

○ 21.TUESDAY

○ 22.WEDNESDAY

TO DO

○ 23.THURSDAY

○ 24.FRIDAY

○ 25.SATURDAY / 26.SUNDAY

July

07/27/20 to 08/02/20

○ 27. MONDAY

PRIORITIES

_____
_____
_____
_____
_____
_____

○ 28. TUESDAY

○ 29. WEDNESDAY

TO DO

_____
_____
_____

○ 30. THURSDAY

_____
_____
_____
_____

○ 31 FRIDAY

_____
_____
_____
_____
_____

○ 1 SATURDAY / 2 SUNDAY

_____
_____
_____
_____

August 2020

Sunday	Monday	Tuesday	Wednesday	Thursday	Friday	Saturday
26	27	28	29	30	31	1
2	3	4	5	6	7	8
9	10	11	12	13	14	15
16	17	18	19	20	21	22
23	24	25	26	27	28	29
30	31	1	2	3	4	5

"Move out of your comfort zone. You can only grow if you are willing to feel awkward and uncomfortable when you try something new." ~Brian Tracy

August

Week 32

08/03/20 to 08/09/20

○ 3.MONDAY

○ 4.TUESDAY

○ 5.WEDNESDAY

○ 6.THURSDAY

○ 7.FRIDAY

○ 8.SATURDAY / 9.SUNDAY

PRIORITIES

TO DO

August

08/10/20 to 08/16/20

○ 10 MONDAY

PRIORITIES

○ 11 TUESDAY

○ 12 WEDNESDAY

TO DO

○ 13 THURSDAY

○ 14 FRIDAY

○ 15 SATURDAY / 16 SUNDAY

August

08/17/20 to 08/23/20

○ 17.MONDAY

PRIORITIES

○ 18.TUESDAY

○ 19.WEDNESDAY

TO DO

○ 20.THURSDAY

○ 21.FRIDAY

○ 22.SATURDAY / 23.SUNDAY

August

08/24/20 to 08/30/20

○ 24.MONDAY

PRIORITIES

○ 25.TUESDAY

○ 26.WEDNESDAY

TO DO

○ 27.THURSDAY

○ 28.FRIDAY

○ 29.SATURDAY / 30.SUNDAY

August

○ 31 MONDAY

PRIORITIES

○ 1 TUESDAY

○ 2 WEDNESDAY

TO DO

○ 3 THURSDAY

○ 4. FRIDAY

○ 5. SATURDAY / 6 SUNDAY

September 2020

Sunday	Monday	Tuesday	Wednesday	Thursday	Friday	Saturday
30	31	1	2	3	4	5
6	7	8	9	10	11	12
13	14	15	16	17	18	19
20	21	22	23	24	25	26
27	28	29	30	1	2	3

"Try not to become a man of success, but a man of value."
~Albert Einstein

September

○ 7.MONDAY

PRIORITIES

○ 8.TUESDAY

○ 9.WEDNESDAY

TO DO

○ 10.THURSDAY

○ 11.FRIDAY

○ 12.SATURDAY / 13.SUNDAY

September

○ 14.MONDAY

○ 15.TUESDAY

○ 16.WEDNESDAY

○ 17.THURSDAY

○ 18.FRIDAY

○ 19.SATURDAY / 20.SUNDAY

September

○ 21 MONDAY

PRIORITIES

○ 22. TUESDAY

○ 23. WEDNESDAY

TO DO

○ 24. THURSDAY

○ 25. FRIDAY

○ 26. SATURDAY / 27. SUNDAY

September

Week 40

○ 28. MONDAY

○ 29. TUESDAY

○ 30. WEDNESDAY

○ 1 THURSDAY

○ 2. FRIDAY

○ 3. SATURDAY / 4. SUNDAY

PRIORITIES

TO DO

October 2020

Sunday	Monday	Tuesday	Wednesday	Thursday	Friday	Saturday
27	28	29	30	1	2	3
4	5	6	7	8	9	10
11	12	13	14	15	16	17
18	19	20	21	22	23	24
25	26	27	28	29	30	31

"Happy are those who dream dreams and are ready to pay the price to make them come true." ~Leon J. Suenes

October

○ 5. MONDAY

PRIORITIES

○ 6. TUESDAY

○ 7. WEDNESDAY

TO DO

○ 8. THURSDAY

○ 9. FRIDAY

○ 10. SATURDAY / 11. SUNDAY

October

○ 12 MONDAY

PRIORITIES

○ 13 TUESDAY

○ 14 WEDNESDAY

TO DO

○ 15 THURSDAY

○ 16 FRIDAY

○ 17 SATURDAY / 18 SUNDAY

October

10/19/20 to 10/25/20

○ 19.MONDAY

PRIORITIES

○ 20.TUESDAY

○ 21.WEDNESDAY

TO DO

○ 22.THURSDAY

○ 23.FRIDAY

○ 24.SATURDAY / 25.SUNDAY

October

○ 26. MONDAY

PRIORITIES

○ 27. TUESDAY

○ 28. WEDNESDAY

TO DO

○ 29. THURSDAY

○ 30. FRIDAY

○ 31 SATURDAY / 1 SUNDAY

November 2020

Sunday	Monday	Tuesday	Wednesday	Thursday	Friday	Saturday
1	2	3	4	5	6	7
8	9	10	11	12	13	14
15	16	17	18	19	20	21
22	23	24	25	26	27	28
29	30	1	2	3	4	5

_____

_____

_____

_____

"Winning isn't everything, but wanting to win is."
~Vince Lombardi

November

Week 45

○ 2.MONDAY

○ 3.TUESDAY

○ 4.WEDNESDAY

○ 5.THURSDAY

○ 6.FRIDAY

○ 7.SATURDAY / 8.SUNDAY

PRIORITIES

TO DO

November

11/09/20 to 11/15/20

○ 9.MONDAY

PRIORITIES

○ 10.TUESDAY

○ 11.WEDNESDAY

TO DO

○ 12.THURSDAY

○ 13.FRIDAY

○ 14.SATURDAY / 15.SUNDAY

November

○ 16 MONDAY

PRIORITIES

○ 17. TUESDAY

○ 18 WEDNESDAY

TO DO

○ 19. THURSDAY

○ 20. FRIDAY

○ 21 SATURDAY / 22 SUNDAY

November

○ 23. MONDAY

PRIORITIES

_____

_____

_____

_____

_____

○ 24. TUESDAY

_____

_____

_____

○ 25. WEDNESDAY

TO DO

_____

_____

○ 26. THURSDAY

_____

_____

_____

_____

○ 27. FRIDAY

_____

_____

_____

_____

_____

○ 28. SATURDAY / 29. SUNDAY

_____

_____

_____

_____

November

○ 30. MONDAY

PRIORITIES

○ 1. TUESDAY

○ 2. WEDNESDAY

TO DO

○ 3. THURSDAY

○ 4. FRIDAY

○ 5. SATURDAY / 6. SUNDAY

December 2020

Sunday	Monday	Tuesday	Wednesday	Thursday	Friday	Saturday
29	30	1	2	3	4	5
6	7	8	9	10	11	12
13	14	15	16	17	18	19
20	21	22	23	24	25	26
27	28	29	30	31	1	2

"Fuck being broke. FBB baby!" ~Ben Stokes III

December

12/07/20 to 12/13/20

○ 7.MONDAY

PRIORITIES

○ 8.TUESDAY

○ 9.WEDNESDAY

TO DO

○ 10.THURSDAY

○ 11.FRIDAY

○ 12.SATURDAY / 13.SUNDAY

December

○ 14.MONDAY

PRIORITIES

○ 15.TUESDAY

○ 16.WEDNESDAY

TO DO

○ 17.THURSDAY

○ 18.FRIDAY

○ 19.SATURDAY / 20.SUNDAY

December

○ 21 MONDAY

PRIORITIES

○ 22. TUESDAY

○ 23. WEDNESDAY

TO DO

○ 24. THURSDAY

○ 25. FRIDAY

○ 26. SATURDAY / 27 SUNDAY

December

○ 28. MONDAY

PRIORITIES

○ 29. TUESDAY

○ 30. WEDNESDAY

TO DO

○ 31. THURSDAY

○ 1. FRIDAY

○ 2. SATURDAY / 3. SUNDAY

54397262R00060

Made in the USA
San Bernardino,
CA